HOW TO
SUCCEED
AT YOUR NEXT
AUDITION

Jessica Neighbor

HOW TO SUCCEED
AT YOUR NEXT
AUDITION

An Interactive Guide
For Performers Ages 12-18

Jessica Neighbor

Contents

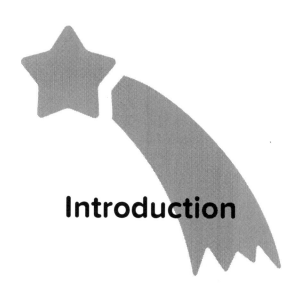

Introduction

Are you a Rising Star Performer?

Are you a young singer or actor who LOVES to perform? Do you want to learn more about the inside secrets and useful strategies to succeed at your audition?

I will teach you that auditions are a game and I'll show you how to succeed at them! Not only will I show you how to succeed at auditions, but I will show you how these lessons will last you a lifetime.

This coaching plan I will teach you in this training book is the exact same one that I use with my private VIP performers who have a 90% audition success rate. I have developed this plan over the past twenty years of coaching successful vocalists, actors, and musical theatre performers on how to feel more confident and succeed at their auditions using my **Audition Skills Interactive Coaching Plan.**

The Audition Skills Interactive Coaching Plan will show you how to...

- **Be completely prepared for your next audition** with my step-by-step audition method guide.

- **Feel more confident** with my **positive mindset training**

which includes video tutorials, scripts, checklists, and worksheets. You can access these interactive tools in my **Book Bonus Encore Page (http://jessicaneighbor.com/ book-bonuses)**

- **Talk to the judges and be your authentic self** with professional industry insider advice and interview coaching practice.

- **Stand out and shine** using your "secret weapon talent" which you'll discover in this book.

- **Create your "Dream Team"** to support you practically and emotionally.

- **Be a positive performance parent** to best support your rising star performer.

About Coach Jessica

Jessica Neighbor is a popular audition and voice coach with over 20 years teaching experience. She owns The Jessica Neighbor Vocal Studio (www.jessicaneighbor.com) in Oakland, California where she coaches talented rising star performers for vocal and dramatic high stake auditions. Jessica coaches one-to-one private sessions in person and by video for performers in The San Francisco Bay Area, Los Angeles, New York City, and International locations. She also offers an online audition training course for performers with private live video coaching.

A Berkeley, California native, Jessica studied vocal and theatrical performance in Berkeley High's prestigious Music Department, and in the competitive **UCLA Theater Program**. She has performed for over 20 years as a lead vocalist in professional musical theater and music ensembles in Los Angeles and The San Francisco Bay Area. She has served on the vocal faculty of **The California Jazz Conservatory in Berkeley, CA** and is a member of **NATS**, The National Association of Teachers of Singing, and is a recipient of the **California State Scholar for The Arts in Theatre Award.** She lives in Oakland with her husband and two sons.

CHAPTER 1
Getting Started

What is your performance dream? What kind of performer do you aspire to become in your life? What are your performance dreams? To star in a musical, sing in a band, or get into a competitive drama or vocal program?

I always ask each of my rising star performers what their aspirations (goals) and inspirations (motivation) are, so that we can unlock their performance passion and purpose. We discover their ultimate goal and then work backwards from there.

Once you identify your performance goal, then you must put yourself "out there" to start playing the performance game to achieve your goal. The gateway to your performance dream is **the audition.**

What is an audition?

An audition, simply put, is a chance to show your talent to the people who make decisions about talent. You get to give them a sample of your talent and leave them wanting more.

Auditions are required for all areas of the performing arts. For example, if you are a singer, then you would sing a song at your audition for a role in music or musical theatre. Or, if you are an actor, then you would act out a monologue or read a scene at your audition to be cast in a play or a movie. You may also have an audition to gain acceptance into an academic performance program. These are all examples of auditions and each area of the performing arts requires auditions including drama, dance, music, modeling, and singing, just to name a few. Rising Stars in all of these performing arts will need to audition in their emphasis, and "Triple Threat Rising Stars" will audition in the three areas of singing, acting, and dancing.

It's particularly important for a "rising star" talent to audition well so that you have as many performance opportunities as possible. The key to becoming a good performer is through performing- a lot. The last thing we want is for an audition to intimidate or hold back a rising star from realizing their full potential.

WHY DO YOU HAVE TO AUDITION?

An audition is like an interview for a performer. At your audition, you usually have a short amount of time to present a memorized piece of material to the judges. It's not enough to talk about your talent, you must demonstrate your skills to show that you are talented. The goal is to get a good role in a play, a movie, or be accepted into a performance program. The judges are usually skilled at choosing the right performers for the particular show or production. A judge or Casting Director's main job is to find the best talent for a role. So, the audition is your chance to show your true, one-of-a-kind talent!

Auditions can bring up nerves and anxieties in performers because they feel they are being judged- and they are. Remember, it's your talent that is being judged and not your whole entire being. I remember being a young performer and feeling so rejected when I did not get an acting or singing part which I wanted. Very often, I was up against many other talented performers and it really came down to who the judges saw as the best fit for the role. We don't know why judges make the decisions they do, all you can do is be yourself and do your best work.

Some young performers might believe the myth that "If I was really talented, then I would not have to audition, I would just be discovered". This myth is like the prince or princess fantasy, where a handsome prince/princess comes along, scoops you up onto his/her horse, and you ride off into the sunset together and live happily ever after. In the performing arts, the happily ever after is the process and not a fixed result. Every performer, no matter their talent level or popularity, has to audition and continue to audition for their entire career. It is part of your job to audition for each new project. Really, it's a good thing.

What if there were no auditions and performers just got roles based on who they knew? Like a messed up popularity contest? Well, that may happen once in a rare case, but the proof is in the pudding- are they any good? Real talent will carry you far if you persist at auditioning and develop your audition skills. All talented performers have to get comfortable with the reality that they must audition. The more comfortable you get at auditioning, the more roles you will get.

Take action now with my **audition goal worksheet in the Book Bonus Encore Page (http://jessicaneighbor.com/book-bo-nuses)**. Get clear about why you want to audition in the first place. A well-known Casting Director said that she can always tell which performers are clear about their audition goals. I give this worksheet to my private VIP audition performers at the beginning of their coaching. This is an excellent exercise to get clear about WHY you are auditioning in the first place. Have fun with this worksheet, it's your chance to dive deep into your feelings and goals for your audition.

If you have a particular show that you are going out for, then you can use that specific audition as your goal for this worksheet. If you don't have a particular audition right now, then I encourage you to imagine what kind of audition you would like to go out for in the future: Broadway, Music Concerts, a High School Musical, Movies, or a College Program, are just some examples. Dream big!

CHAPTER 1 WRAP-UP:

1. **Auditions are your first step** to getting into a performance production. You prepare audition material, like a song or monologue, for the audition and you try to do your best work in front of the Judges. Remember, you always want to leave them wanting MORE!

2. **Remember that every performer, brand new or famous, must audition for their entire performance career.** You may as well learn to like auditioning because you'll be doing it a lot.

3. **Lights, Camera, Action:** Next, take the first step for your audition success and fill out my worksheet, **"Audition Goals"** in the **Book Bonus Encore Page (http://jessica-neighbor.com/book-bonuses)**.

CHAPTER 2:
Research Your Audition like a Pro

- What you need to research to shine at your next audition.
- Common mistakes performers make when researching auditions.
- My Audition Research Checklist to get you ready.

Do you want to shine at your next audition? The first step towards your audition success, long before your actual audition day, is doing your audition research ahead of time. Doing your research is a huge part of getting in to your audition. Many performers skip this crucial step and wind up hurting their chances.

For instance, if you have an audition coming up in one month and the audition guidelines have just been posted, do you take the time to read through all of the audition instructions, even the small print? Absolutely! Doing your research shows that you are taking the production seriously and putting in thoughtful time to know all that you can in advance about the audition. Casting directors share with me the mistakes that performers made at their auditions because they did not do their research. It cost these talented performers their chance to perform, get the part, and a chance to truly shine.

If your audition guidelines says to choose a pop vocal piece that is less than one minute, then that is what you must do. Don't think that you can be an exception to the rule, the rules are there for a good reason. If the audition says to bring in three copies of sheet music, then you must follow this exact instruction. If you don't understand the instructions, don't be afraid to ask an associate for the answer. They would much rather have you ask than show up unprepared at the audition and waste everyone's time. If you do your research and make the right choices for your audition, you are already shining before you even walk through the audition door!

Doing your research will also be your first step to feeling more confident and will help your positive mindset for your audition. The more you know about what to expect, the more calm you will feel going into that new environment. Never guess at the guidelines, always seek out clarification.

Let me give you one of my own audition experiences where I am so relieved that I did my audition research to avoid getting humiliated and score an audition win:

I was studying theater at UCLA and a competitive audition came up for an exclusive film acting class in the film department with a tough acting coach. A lot of my friends and I were excited to try out for the class and gain experience about how to act in front of the camera and meet some of the directors in the film department.

I was taking a Shakespeare acting class at that time and I was absolutely in love with Shakespeare prose, so I decided to audition using a classical monologue from one of his plays. Since there were no clear guidelines posted for the film acting class audition, I double checked with the Teacher's Assistant about my audition choice and he started laughing when I told him about my classical audition choice. He said that this coach is a method acting coach who strongly prefers contemporary monologues. I asked him for some suggestions and I wound up using one of his recommended monologues. It was a quick turn around, I only had a few days to prepare, but boy am I glad I did.

When the audition day came, we each went into the room individually to audition. The Acting Coach gave me no feedback after my audition, she simply said, "Bring in the next one". At the end of our auditions, she called all of us back in, around 20-25 actors. She said in a quiet but clear voice, "If I say your name, I want you to run, not walk, but run to the nearest acting coach to learn how to do a proper audition". My jaw dropped, this was so humiliating. As she read the names aloud, some people burst into tears, some stormed off. The handful of us who were left just sat there trying not to move a muscle to draw attention to ourselves. Then she said, "If I have not called your name, class starts next week. You are dismissed". I did not know if I should celebrate or console my classmates who were rejected, but I knew I was so glad to have talked with her TA to get my audition material on point. The class wound up being an interesting and mildly tortuous experience in method acting for film, but I learned a lot from it and met some great directors.

This is just one example of doing your research for an audition to choose the correct material. My **Audition Guideline Checklist Worksheet** in the **Book Bonus Encore Page (http://jessica-neighbor.com/book-bonuses)** will help you make sure that you are covering all of the bases to prepare for your upcoming auditions. It's helpful to know what is and what's not within your control at auditions; doing your research is absolutely within your control and you should take full advantage of knowing as much as possible beforehand.

My Industry Insider Tip: Ask the audition contact person if they have a "recommendation audition material list" if it's an open choice audition. Ask if it is unclear to you what types of songs or monologues you should use. Don't be afraid to ask for help. I always have each of my private students fill out their auditions guidelines to make sure that they are crystal clear about the expectations.

Be sure to use your good common sense about your audition research as well. If the audition is a vocal audition and the producer works with pop stars, then sing a pop song. If you are going out for a role in the musical "Hairspray" and the audition calls for a 2-minute song that is NOT from the musical, then pick a song from the same musical genre and 1960's era.

If the guidelines say to check in 30 minutes before your audition, then do just that! There are very good reasons why auditions have these specific guidelines. You'll get more comfortable with them the more auditions you go out on. At first, just make sure to do your homework. Believe me, the judges will thank you for it.

CHAPTER 2 WRAP-UP:

1. **Your first step to shining bright at your audition is doing your audition research!**

2. **Always follow the audition guidelines** to shine bright before you even walk through the audition door! Have your "Practical Team" help you double check your guidelines, you'll learn more about this team in Chapter 8.

3. **Lights, Camera, Action:** Fill out my **"Rising Star Audition Guidelines"** to make sure that you are crystal clear about the requirements in my **Book Bonus Encore Page (http://jessicaneighbor.com/book-bonuses)**.

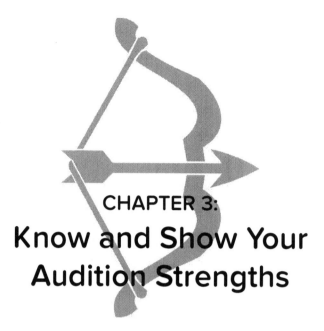

CHAPTER 3:
Know and Show Your
Audition Strengths

KNOW YOUR SECRET WEAPON!

What is your secret weapon? Your secret talent that really helps you stand out? Knowing what your performance strengths are is your best secret weapon! A lot of young rising star performers are still figuring out what they are good at, but performers by age eight, already have clear strengths that are apparent and set them apart. Ask yourself, what are you especially good at in performing? Are you funny? Are you dramatic? Do you love to sing? Are you a great dancer? These are all strengths that you can use to win at your audition!

One of the best gifts you can give yourself is to do what you love, what you are passionate about, and align your talent with your natural abilities. Try not to be all things to all people, do what you love and you will be on the right path.

"WHAT IS MY SECRET WEAPON?" DISCOVERY EXERCISE:

A great exercise to do is to ask your "fan club", those friends and family members who you trust, to share with you what they think are your performance strengths.

You can have them fill out a short questionnaire about you and ask these following questions:

1. What do you like best about my personality?
2. What do you like best about me when I perform?
3. When I perform, what makes me stand out?
4. Which character in a play do I most resemble?
5. If you were to cast me in a play, who would you cast me as?

BE A TRIPLE THREAT

Sometimes auditions require us to get out of our comfort zone and out of our "secret weapon" zone. In these situations, you simply do the best you can. Often times in musical theater, you will have to audition with a song, a dance routine, and a dramatic monologue. This requires you to be a triple threat talent: Someone who can act, sing, and dance. This does not mean that you have to be the best singer-dance-actor triple threat, but you can learn to "accentuate the positive" in each of these areas.

Like maybe you are an incredible vocalist but not as skilled a dancer but you can follow the basic moves and act confident while dancing. You may be required to dance, don't worry, you will probably not be cast as the main dancer. However, by being "good enough" as a dancer and feeling more confident, you'll increase your odds of getting a larger part. If you can master the basics of the triple threat: a singer, dancer, actor, then you will open up so many more role options for yourself.

My Industry Insider Advice: What's your type? Now Break the Mold!

While I was auditioning in LA, I was constantly given the advice to "know my type" as an actor and singer. The problem was that I was good at lots of types of music and acting, and I did not want to typecast myself. I love when my performer clients break down barriers regarding traditional gender and cultural rules and perform in roles that they would not be an obvious "type-cast" for in a traditional sense. I recently saw a production of Mary Poppins at The Berkeley Playhouse where Mary Poppins was fantastic and happened to be African-American. Her talent as a performer overruled the status quo type casting. Other talented performers can be cast as opposite gender roles if they are the best for the role. In this regard, I say go for the moon! Do what you love and go for the parts you desire.

Here are examples of three different performer's secret weapons:

Matthew is hilarious! He can improvise and mimic voices. He has a natural ability to be funny without even trying. He has a quirky, disheveled look that further compliments his comedic talent. He's not trying to be funny, he just is. His audition strength is his humor and he will pick a comedic song and monologue for his audition.

Anna is a dreamer. She has a high, angelic soprano voice that makes her sound like a songbird. She has a kindness that exudes from her smile and she has a warm presence on stage. Anna's audition strength is to showcase her lovely voice and kind nature with a song ballad and romantic monologue for her audition.

Sophia is a rebel! She has a gravelly rock voice, looks cool, like she's the singer in a band, and she says little but communicates a lot with her eyes and voice. Sophia's audition strength is her rock voice and strong stage persona. She will choose a rock song and bold heroine monologue for her audition.

Do you see how all three performers above each have their

special performance secret weapon? They are being themselves, this is what comes naturally to them.

Now, it's your turn to discover and identify what comes easily to you. Knowing your strengths will help you in selecting the best audition material for you, as explained in detail in chapter 6. Often when you are starting out, I think it's great to go out on most auditions and not get discouraged if you are not always the right type. Remember, you are developing your audition muscle. Over time, you will get stronger at auditions and at knowing and highlighting your unique strengths.

CHAPTER 3 WRAP-UP:

1. **Identify what your performance strengths** are and make sure to showcase those strengths at your audition. Ask your "fans" for feedback, we'll learn more about your fans in Chapter 8.

2. **Try to be a well-rounded triple threat** performer to open up the most opportunities. You don't have to be the best at each of these talents, just be good enough.

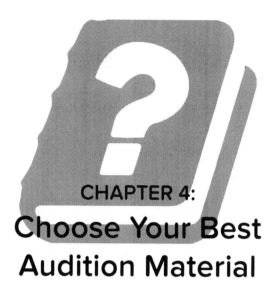

CHAPTER 4:
Choose Your Best Audition Material

C hoosing audition material that best suits you, will make an enormous difference for your audition. An important part of my job as a private audition coach is to help identify the audition material that is the best fit for my performers. I am always looking for that audition material that helps them shine the brightest. It's a process to find that best material, but with my selection guide in this chapter, you will find your strongest material so that you just blow the judges away!

For the first step in selecting material, I will have performers bring in 3-5 audition songs or monologues to perform for me, so that we can choose their best piece that really makes them shine the brightest.

Performers need to be objective about selecting their material. Try not to choose material just because you like it, choose it because it's truly a good fit for your talent. It's very important at this stage to get help from your "performance team", either an audition coach, a teacher, or a trusted friend, who can give you their honest opinion about your best material choice.Here is my audition selection strategy for both a vocal audition and a dramatic audition:

HOW TO CHOOSE YOUR BEST VOCAL AUDITION SONG

ASK YOURSELF THESE THREE QUESTIONS:

Question 1: Is this song a good reflection of who I am as a performer? What type of performer are you? The sweet ingénue, the bluesy belter, or the silly comic? What parts have you been cast in previously? The Good Witch or the Wicked Witch in the Wizard of Oz? A good song of any musical genre, whether it's musical theater, Jazz or Pop, should have a strong point of view. You want to choose a song that speaks to you, that moves you, that motivates you to practice it and perform it wholeheartedly. Your audition song is your magic weapon; choose the one that makes you feel invincible.

Now Question 2: Is this song comfortable for my vocal range and vocal style? You want your song to fit you like a well-tailored suit or gown. Is your song comfortable for you to sing? If you are allowed to transpose the music, do you need to change the key and is this allowed for this audition? Your audition song should be in your comfort range with a few stretches to demonstrate your vocal dynamics such as a few high notes on the bridge. You do not want the majority of your song to be a stretch; don't make an audition harder than it already is. Pick a medium difficult song, not an easy song that is too simple, or a difficult song that intimidates you, but a comfortable song with a few vocal challenges. On a scale of 1-10 with 10 being the most difficult, where does your song fall? You want your song to be around a 6-7 in the difficulty scale.

The other part of question 2 relates to your vocal style. Pick a song that suits your vocal timbre. Think of your voice as a horn- what kind of horn are you? A high flute or a deep tuba? Think of the songs and singers that best flatter your natural vocal tone. Pick a song with a vocal style that feels natural and authentic to your voice.

Question 3: Is this song appropriate for this specific audition? Make sure that your song reflects the spirit of the audition and is appropriate for the production or program. If you are applying to a Jazz program, sing a Jazz song. If you hear from other singers that the judges prefer Musical Theater, do Musical Theater. Make sure you are flexible enough to choose a song that is a good fit for this particular audition, plus the best fit for your voice. Remember, research the guidelines for the audition and ask for specific song recommendations from the program if possible.

These three questions will help you in selecting a great song. There is no other voice in the world exactly like yours, so choose a song that really brings out your authentic voice. Have fun exploring!

How to Choose Your Best Monologue

Choosing a good monologue is very important. I recommend that performers have at least 4 monologues memorized for different kinds of auditions. The main categories are:

Contemporary Comedic: This monologue should be from a modern published play and showcase your comedic strengths.

Contemporary Dramatic: This monologue should be from a modern published play and should demonstrate your dramatic, more serious strengths.

Classic Comedic: This monologue type will be from a classic piece such as Shakespeare.

Classic Dramatic: This monologue type will be from a classic piece like Shakespeare and demonstrate your classic dramatic/ serious abilities.

Now, ask yourself what acting style you have experience performing: classical, modern, dramatic or comedy? Remember to draw on your "Secret Weapon" strengths that we went over in Chapter 3. Choose the monologue category that feels the most natural to you to perform. Make sure your monologue is age-ap-propriate and compliments your natural abilities.

My Industry Insider Tip about Monologues: Finding monologues can be tricky, especially for younger performers, because often, they are excerpts from within a published play and not licensed to appear on the web. There are monologue books but a word of caution, many other young performers are using these same monologue books.

My advice is to watch or read plays and discover monologues that you like from the categories above. There are monologue search engines online as well and a great amount of monologue videos on Youtube that you can use for inspiration.

For some auditions, you can also think outside of the box and recite a monologue from a non-fiction source. I applied and got into NYU Tisch School for the Arts with a monologue from a non-fiction kid's account of her experience in Juvenile Hall. Remember to do your research! More often, auditions require monologues from published plays. Beware of the "free monologues" that are written by the same person online, these can be frowned upon. Do not write your own monologue unless the guidelines state to do so or you are a published playwright.

A talented actor/writer friend of mine told me how she was signed with her first casting agent. She went in for her audition with her monologue prepared. After she finished, the agent asked her if she knew another monologue. And another. After she did five monologues, the agent accepted her! It took the forethought on my friend's part to have that many pieces prepared. Remember that monologues and audition songs are just a sample of your talent. Be ready to have several different samples ready to perform. Always have at least a plan A and B audition piece ready for each audition.

CHAPTER 4 WRAP-UP:

1. Get a short list of audition material and perform it in front of your "performance team" to choose your strongest choice. Always have a plan B choice as well.

2. Use my vocal song audition guideline in this chapter when choosing a song.

3. Use my monologue guidelines in this chapter when choosing a monologue.

4. **Lights, Camera, Action:** Watch my video tutorial, **"How to Choose Your Best Audition Material"** in The **Book Bonus Encore Page (http://jessicaneighbor.com/book-bonuses)**

CHAPTER 5:
Feel Your Most Confident for Your Audition

My positive mindset training is a simple and effective method to help you feel calm and positive at auditions. I use this training with my private rising star performers who have high stake auditions and feel very nervous and want to feel more confident. This is a huge part of my private coaching.

A lot of performers struggle with the emotional/psychological part of auditions. Why? Out of the many reasons, the main one I have seen over the past 20 years in my coaching practice is that performers worry too much about the things that are out of their control at auditions.

It's very natural to worry about things like, "Will they like me?" or "What if I mess up?" or, "What if I'm not good enough"? These fears and worries can take on a life of their own and get in our way at our audition. In fact, these fears can ruin our chances at succeeding at auditions if we don't learn to control them.

The truth is that there are many things out of our control, but we do have things within our control that can make a huge difference at increasing our odds of succeeding at auditions and the number one thing we have control over is our mindset.

In addition to the normal worries and fears that come along with auditions, Rising Star performers are at a heightened self-aware age and self-conscious stage of their development which can make the experience of auditioning much more daunting. I like to show young rising stars that you can use your self-awareness as a positive, rather than a negative. Being aware of yourself is actually an asset for how you can best present yourself to the judges. It's a balance between being self-aware enough, but not so much so that you are guarded and closed off. Through the mindset training, physical and mental exercises, you will feel more grounded, confident, and comfortable at your auditions.

Let's meet Eva. She is a composite of many different talented rising stars who I have coached. Eva will show you many of the mis-steps you can make during your audition process. Perhaps you have made some of these same mistakes before? I sure know I did early on in my performance career!

EVA'S AUDITION STORY

"Eva has a big audition for her favorite show. This is her favorite musical ever since she was a little girl and she has the chance to try out for her all-time favorite role in the musical production at a Repertory Theatre Company. Eva is pumped! Eva is so excited that she jumps right into preparing her favorite song from the show for her audition. What she fails to notice is that the audition guidelines state NOT to sing a song from the actual play- Eva does not read the audition guidelines closely enough.

Eva starts telling everyone about her upcoming audition and her friends and family, her "fans", get excited for her. They tell her that she'd be perfect for the role and that she should go for it- just the encouragement she needs. Except that now, her friends are asking about the upcoming audition all the time and it's starting to feel like too much pressure for Eva.

To manage this pressure, Eva begins to distract herself with other things besides practicing her audition song material. She does practice occasionally, but her fears start to come up every time she practices and they start to overwhelm her, so she leaves her room and goes to do something, anything else.

Then Eva starts to feel guilty about not practicing enough, which makes her want to avoid practicing even more. When she does practice, she runs her song the same way each time and forgets a few lyrics, but she figures that she'll have her song fully memorized by the audition date.

Her Mom, her "support team", asks her about her practice and points out that she's concerned that Eva is not practicing enough. Eva feels bad but her Mom just annoys her, they have an argument, and her Mom feels shut out of her process. After a few attempts to get Eva to practice, her Mom gives up and figures Eva will either sink or swim on her own.

As her audition day approaches, she starts to doubt herself and wonders if she should even go through with it. She spends more time worrying about her audition, instead of practicing for it!

Finally, her audition day arrives and she feels out of sorts. She did not sleep well the night before and she feels foggy headed. She scrambles to get dressed and changes her outfit 10 times. She looks at her clock and realizes that she has to get to her audition fast, so she skips breakfast.

When she arrives at her audition, she is rushing and harassed and signs up in the last slot available that day. Eva is now stuck in the waiting room for hours before her audition slot time. She can hear the other singers through the audition room door and they sound really good! She gets even more nervous and starts to sweat and shake.

She did not pack her audition care package, full of healthy snacks, water, and fun things to do to lift her spirits. She has no snack, no water, and she's last on the list, yikes!

Finally, it's her turn to go into the audition room. She's feeling light headed from not eating, but she pushes through. As she enters the room, she is surprised to see not one judge as she imagined in her head, but FIVE judges!

The judge in the center says hello and reads over her headshot and resume. He asks if she has any questions before she begins. She realizes that she really needs to use the bathroom, so she asks if she can go. He agrees, but he looks annoyed. When she returns, two of the judges are now missing. One is writing in her notebook and does not even raise her head.

Eva asks if she can start. They say yes and she starts to sing a cappella, but she forgets to do her slate. She starts off fine but when she gets to her bridge, she struggles to remember her lyrics. She had hoped to have her song memorized, but she's feeling way more nervous than she expected and she just can't remember her bridge lyrics.

Eva stops singing, she says sorry and asks to start again. They say OK and she starts again, but this time she starts in a higher key and now she is straining to reach her highest notes. The shirt she chose turns out to feel itchy and she has an urge to scratch the small of her back during her entire song.

The judge in the center cuts her off before her song ends, she does not even get to her big ending- her favorite and best section of her song. She is stunned that it's over so fast. She stands there blinking and looking at the judges. They simply say, "Thank You, that will be all" and wait for her to leave. She is so shocked that she forgets to thank them and quickly rushes out of the room.

In the waiting room, she feels a well of emotions start to rise up in her throat and she starts to cry. She feels bad, embarrassed, and she is not quite sure why.

Three days later, the audition results are posted and Eva's name does not appear on the list. She feels devastated and now she has to tell all of her friends that she did not get in. Eva feels discouraged. Her best friend tells her that she's proud of Eva for trying out. Eva should feel proud, but she does not and she can't figure out exactly why."

LET'S REVIEW WHAT MISSTEPS EVA MADE FOR HER AUDITION, SO SHE KNOWS BETTER FOR NEXT TIME:

1. **Eva forgot to do her audition research**: Eva forgot to research her audition, so she chose the wrong material. The audition guidelines stated to pick a song that was not from the show but she did not take the time to fully read over them.

2. **She did not make a practice plan:** Eva let her nerves get in the way of her practice. She did not practice consistently enough to thoroughly master her audition material, so that she would feel confident. She memorized her piece but not deeply enough to remember her lyrics under pressure.

3. **She did not have an audition schedule plan:** Eva did not take care of herself the night before her audition to be ready the next morning. She should have picked out her outfit ahead of time, she could have avoided that scratchy shirt and the 10 outfit changes! She also could have made sure to have a relaxed night to rest herself for her audition the next morning.

4. **Her worries got the best of her:** Her nerves started to overwhelm her and take over her talent. She could use **Positive Mindset Training to have more positive tools** like an **audition mantra** to calm down, breathing techniques to center herself, and she could create a **self-care audition kit,** that you will learn about and be sure to bring to your next audition!

5. **She did not give herself a good morning:** Eva should have woken up early enough to give herself time to get ready and eat a healthy breakfast. Instead, she had to rush which made her feel stressed-out. When you give yourself enough time to get ready for yourself in the morning, you will feel more calm and confident when you arrive at your audition.

6. **She did not follow the standard audition etiquette:** At her audition, she came late and made a bad first impression. She had to sign-up in the last time slot. She forgot to use the bathroom and then wasted some of her audition time and the judges' time. She made the mistake of apologizing to the judges when she made a mistake which performers never want to do. Eva forgot to introduce herself (do her slate) or thank them at the end. **She did do her audition, which is great, but she did it all wrong.**

   If she had started off with positive mindset training, Eva could have set herself up for success. I take each of my students through the full training process, so that they know what to expect and can best prepare for it time wise, practice wise, and often most importantly, prepare mentally with my positive mindset training.

Your Positive Outcome Worksheet Exercise

Now that you read about Eva's mistakes, it's your turn to write out your worst fears and greatest hopes for your future audition. In this next worksheet exercise, you will dive into what could go right and wrong at your next audition. This exercise is a great way to contain your fears on paper and to state your positive outcome, so you can see it and then actually make it happen for yourself! You can get your **Positive Outcome Worksheet** in **The Book Bonus Encore Page (http://jessicaneighbor.com/book-bonuses)**

Very often in my coaching, I'm teaching performers how to get out of their own way. We all have habits that are actually hurting our performances, instead of helping them. Let's identify the main things that can get in our way:

1. Your Busy Body:

In my summer audition coaching program intensive for my "triple threat" students in summer 2016, we discussed what it means to really feel confident onstage. We talked a lot about what can get in our way of feeling confident and what can help us to feel more confident when we perform.

The performers agreed that practice and feeling prepared made them feel the most confident. They also agreed that their nerves made them feel the least confident. So we addressed their nerves and how nerves come out in our performance: Rushing our lines, sweaty palms, an accelerated heart rate, feeling uncomfortable in their own skin. We worked on how to calm our nerves in our physical body and in our mind.

How to Calm Your Body: One effective way to increase confidence is through your physical body and your body awareness. Where do you hold your tension? Are you aware of your body during your performances? At my program, we had to settle a lot of "busy hands" and "busy feet" during camp rehearsals that were detracting from otherwise wonderful performances. You will learn about how to calm and center your busy body in my body awareness tutorial videos in Chapter 6.

2. Your Inner Heckler

The other key to feel confident is to understand your emotions. How do you feel about yourself emotionally while onstage? Do you have an "inner heckler" that won't be quiet during your show? Do they whisper things to you like, "You are no good" or, "You look like a fool right now"? One student pointed out that her inner heckler would probably look like the grumpy puppets from The Muppet Show, Statler and Waldorf. This image of the grumpy puppets up in the box seats yelling out insults during the show is so great for putting a funny face on the distracting voices in our own head!

How to Quiet Your Inner Heckler: The first step to take on your inner heckler is to not believe what they are saying to you. Their voice is the worried part of yourself that turns inward. We are actually beating ourselves up emotionally- ouch! Most creative people do have an inner heckler and in small doses, they can encourage us to grow. It's good to be a little self-critical, the key word here being "a little". Some performers have this inner critic more than others. I have a pretty large inner heckler who I have learned to keep in check. I definitely don't believe what my inner-heckler says any longer, and I've created a counter voice to further boost my spirits: **My inner number one fan!**

3. Your Inner #1 fan:

It's not enough to ignore or turn down our inner-heckler, we need to turn up our positive internal voice that I lovingly call your inner number one fan. We need to love ourselves, we need to believe in ourselves, just like an adoring fan loves their favorite singer or actor. Try to imagine how good you would feel if you believed in yourself as much as you believe in a star who has already made it! When you hear successful performers talk, they often say that they always believed in themselves. This is not to say that they did not have self-doubt or worry too, but they had a deep rooted belief that they could make it!

4. YOUR WORRY WORM:

Your worry worm is that part of you that worries too much about your audition. Your worry worm is different from your inner-heckler because it's not mean spirited, it just makes you nervous and distracted from doing your best. Typical worry worm thoughts are, "What if I forget my lines?" or "What if the judges don't like me" or "What if I mess up"?

How to Calm down your Worry Worm: These are all real worries but there is a simple way to put that worry worm back in its hole! Remind yourself that you have practiced enough, that you are prepared, and even if you mess up, you are going to be OK.

See, the worry worm is actually an ancient tool for survival that helped us to be safe around deadly threats like bears or snakes. By being a little worried, our ancestors avoided getting eaten alive! The problem with the ancient worry worm is that there are no bears or snakes at your audition, but it still worries that you will get hurt. You must remind your worry worm that you'll be OK, that it's just an audition, and that this will not break you. We have to sooth our worry worm and let it know that you are going to be OK no matter what happens. This way, you will avoid going into the "fight or flight" primal response with your nervous system that will get all kinds of icky things going in your body like dry mouth, sweaty palms, shaking, and even hyper-ventilating. No way do you want that at your audition. You want to feel calm, centered, and ready to handle anything.

CHAPTER 5 WRAP-UP:

1. **Mental roadblocks** can prevent us from doing our best at our audition.

2. **Eva's Audition** shows you what not to do at your next audition.

3. Your **Worry Worm** and **Inner Heckler** can flare up when you audition.

4. Your **Inner-Number One Fan** will keep you feeling positive.

5. **Lights, Camera, Action:** Fill out your **Positive Outlook Audition Worksheet** in the **Book Bonus Encore Page** (http://jessicaneighbor.com/book-bonuses)

CHAPTER 6:
Master Your Audition Material and Make Practice Fun!

1. Section 1: How to memorize your material.

2. Section 2: How to have good body language.

3. Section 3: How to make practice fun.

In this first section, we will explore how you can deeply memorize and know your audition material so well that you don't forget a line, and so you feel your most confident, even when you are under a lot of pressure at your audition. A very common mistake performers make in preparing for their audition is to not memorize your material deeply enough. We can store information in our short-term or long- term memory. You want to aim to memorize your piece well enough so that you have it stored securely in your long-term memory. You want to have your monologue, or song, and plan b material, so thoroughly memorized, that you are absolutely certain about every word.

A lot of unexpected things can come up at our auditions that can distract us, and if we don't have our material fully memorized, then we can get ourselves into deep trouble.

REMEMBER, MEMORIZING AND MASTERING YOUR MATERIAL IS SOMETHING THAT YOU HAVE FULL CONTROL OVER.

There can be time pressure auditions where we have short notice to prepare. In these situations, you practice as much as you can in a pinch and your practice skills that we'll go over in this chapter will help you even in a rush audition situation.

The bottom line is that you will know when you fully have something memorized, and furthermore you want to have your material "mastered". I love the word "mastered" because it means that you are in control, you are totally confident in your abilities, which is exactly how you need to feel going into an audition. "Kind of, or sort of" memorizing a song or monologue is not enough. That will hurt you at your audition. Remember how "Eva" put off memorizing her song section, the bridge, in her audition material and assumed that she'd just somehow figure it out? Well she did not figure it out because she did not put in the time and she fell apart at her audition.

Here are my coaching strategies for how to memorize and master your audition material, so you can ace your audition!

MY 6 STEPS TO MASTERING YOUR MATERIAL:

Step 1: Print out your song lyrics & sheet music, and/or monologue that you will be memorizing. You want to have all of your material written out in an easy to find location like a notebook or online in a document folder, so you can easily access and refer back to your written material. Keep your master copies clean and take care of your material. Make a copy that you will write notes on for your practice. It's not enough to bookmark material online, you want to print it out so you can take it with you anywhere you go.

Step 2: Memorize your material in small sections of 2-4 lines per section. Memorize your material using the "chunking" method by learning a little at a time. This way, you allow your mind to fully memorize small sections without overloading yourself. Have fun with your memorization, you are learning an author's beautiful words that they spent months, maybe years, perfecting. Give yourself the time and space to learn your material in a light, fun, non-crammed way. Do not go to the next section until you fully memorize the section before. Add on sections until you have the whole song or monologue memorized.

Step 3: Write out your lyrics or lines from memory and then check that you got them all right. This is a great exercise because you can self-check your memory. Also, the act of writing down your material will further reinforce your memory strength.

Step 4: Recite your material to your "support team" and have them read along to check your memorization. Remember, this material was written and crafted by an author, it is very important that you show you can master the exact text. It also shows a level of respect that not all young performers appreciate. You will be expected to do the same in the production you are auditioning for, so do it for your audition piece for certain. Have someone prompt you and run it several times, not just once, to ensure that you really have it locked down.

Step 5: Repeat, Repeat, Repeat! Sing your song again and again! Recite your monologue until you can say it in your sleep. Make sure to highlight the sections that that you are still forgetting. Make sure to drill and repeat these sections. When I was preparing to sing the National Anthem for The Giant's Baseball Team at Pac Bell Park Stadium for 40,000 people in San Francisco, California, I drilled The Star Spangled Banner until I could recite it backwards in my sleep. I was so worried that I'd forget the lyrics to our very own National Anthem, so I went above and beyond what I needed to do to feel absolutely certain in my song.

When I was out on the field and up on the pitcher's mound in front of that huge crowd, I felt certain of my lyrics and I was able to be fully present to enjoy this special moment in my singing career. I was nervous for sure, but it was an amazing experience and I'm so glad I put in the effort and time. I also got to hang out with all my friends and family and cheer on our team that day afterwards which was a blast! I could do this because I had put in my preparation time and it paid off!

6. Step 6: Create Visual Memory Cues: For those lyrics that are especially challenging to remember, come up with a visual memory cue in your head for those lyrics. For example, in my

National Anthem performance, I really struggled with the song lyric line,

"O'er the ramparts we watched, were so gallantly streaming".

So my Voice Coach and I came up with a plan. First of all, I had to figure out what the heck a rampart was. "An embankment, a defensive wall in battle". Oh, got it! What's O'er? Oh, it's old English for "over", check. Then I made an image of this stone wall in my mind. But what was "so gallantly streaming? The flag, ah, let's add that flag in my visual memory along with the stone wall. Now when I sing that line, I have a clear image of the grey stone wall with a flag over the top of it waving at sunrise.

SECTION 2: HOW TO HAVE YOUR BEST BODY LANGUAGE

In this section, you can watch my video tutorials to go over what to do with your body at your audition. Your body language communicates a lot about you. Make sure you are showing that you feel confident, prepared, and calm. I have coached hundreds of performers who have nervous habits that get in the way of their performance auditions.

Watch "Best Body Language" Tutorial videos in the Chapter 6 section of Book Bonus Encore Page (http://jessicaneighbor. com/book-bonuses):

1. Watch my tutorial video about "What to do with your eyes".

2. Watch my tutorial video about "What to do with your hands".

When I coach my private students, I always review their body language skills because often performers make common mistakes that distract from their audition performance. The most common body language mistakes are to be either a busy body, or to do the opposite and be too still like a statue. My tutorial videos will show you what to avoid doing with your body and simple exercises to find a good movement plan for you. **Here are the two main physical habits you want to avoid:**

The Stiff Body: I had one student once who was an incredible vocalist, but she just stood there like a deer caught in the headlights;

she was stiff and uncomfortable. For her coaching, I had her do movement exercises to connect more with her physical body. Her issue was that she was too much in her head, her voice was fantastic, but her body and facial expressions did not match. With practice, she was able to make some movement and blocking choices that complimented her voice and helped to further tell her story. She had to get out of her comfort zone, but it was well worth it when she got into her audition for a competitive academic vocal program!

The Busy Body: Another student of mine had the opposite issue. She was a talented musical theatre performer, but she could not stop moving during her songs as if she were the energizer bunny. Her movements were not helping to tell her story when she performed, in fact they were really distracting and made her appear nervous, restless, and uncertain. So her coaching practice with me was all about finding her physical center, and doing movements that only made sense for her musical theatre song. Once she was able to focus her nervous energy and make clear choices about her movements, she nailed her song- and she got the lead in her next musical audition!

SECTION 3: HOW TO MAKE PRACTICE FUN

Ah, practice. This can be a very tricky thing for performers. You may be so enthusiastic to be in a play or show, but the reality of the daily practice requirements can feel like a real burden.

Think like an athlete! Stephen Curry does not feel like showing up to basketball practice every day, but he does so because his team is depending on him. When you get into your play, you will be expected to commit to regular and long rehearsals with the cast. Consider your self-practice for your audition your pre-show rehearsals that are just for you. Many people practice more when they are in a group and that makes sense. But a good group is only as talented as their individual members and each member should be doing their own private practice as well.

The good news is that there is not only one way to practice!

I used to think that I had to labor long and hard over my songs and monologues in order to master them. Yet, I would take it too far and my practice would feel like another chore, and eventually something else to avoid doing. I would vacillate between going overboard in my practice, or not doing it at all. What I realized for me was that doing a practice in consistent, small doses was the best way for me to practice!

Some performers are morning people and practice early, right after they eat breakfast. Others, myself included, are night owls and we get our best practice done after the sun sets.

It's not the quantity of time, but the quality of time that counts in practice. Practicing 20 minutes with good focus is more effective than for 45 minutes without concentrating. It takes a lot to learn new material, and further master it, so give yourself enough focused time and realize when you are no longer feeling productive.

Another important thing to consider is your timeline. Do you have 2 months, 2 weeks, or 2 days to practice for your audition? This will change your approach to how often you need to practice. Make out a practice schedule leading up to your audition day, and try to stick to it. Give yourself a plan B if your initial schedule does not work out. Give yourself one day off each week to relax and restore yourself. Don't go so long in between practices that you start to forget your material.

Make practice fun! The more we stay connected to why we practice for positive reasons, the more we will be motivated to practice! Negative thoughts or punishing practice routines can really break your spirit and take out all the fun of practice.

HERE ARE A FEW THOUGHTS TO KEEP IT LIGHT AND KEEP PRACTICE FUN

Practice is a chance to explore new ways of doing my piece.

I am allowed to make mistakes and take risks when I practice- these will actually help me to grow as a performer.

I like to create a fun environment when I practice. I can put on a costume or music that helps me get into my practice.

I am not looking for quick results in my practice. I know that my skill and talent comes from slow and steady practice.

The more I practice well, the better I'll feel at my audition.
I'm in control of my practice!

The final step of your practice: Develop your character

Once you have fully memorized your material, you are going to want to have fun creating the specific details about your character in your song or monologue. If you are doing a piece from theater, then you will have a lot of information about the character from the play. Always read the full play to understand your material.

If you are doing a pop song that is not from a full play, you will want to create a backstory and a specific song setting for yourself. I would not only rely on the video or what the songwriter may say the song is about, find the pop song's meaning for yourself. Develop your character so that you are clear about the WHY, WHAT, WHO, and WHERE in your audition piece.

CHAPTER 6 WRAP-UP:

1. Use my **"Six Step Memorization Strategy"** so that you have your lyrics and lines on point!

2. **Lights, Camera, Action:** Watch my **Body Language Tutorial Videos** for your eyes, hands, and physical nerves" in the **Book Bonus Encore Page (http://jessicaneighbor.com/ book-bonuses)**

3. Practice: Find the time of day and fun way to practice that keeps you motivated.

CHAPTER 7:
Create Your Best
Audition Portfolio

I t's important for a young rising star performer to have a performance portfolio. Your portfolio is your headshot and resume that you give to the judges at auditions, so they can remember who you are and contact you to cast you in their production. You don't have to spend a ton of money to have a professional portfolio, but you do want to know the industry standard and make an effort because that is like your job resume and it makes a lasting impression.

Here is a list for a typical performance portfolio:

- Your Headshot

- Your Resume

- Your Sheet Music

- Your Showreel/Video

Let's go over each portfolio piece individually, so you understand each piece of your portfolio to make a great first impression:

Your Resume: Your resume is a page with highlights from your performance experience written out. Break your resume into different sections like acting, singing, Film & Television. Make sure to leave room at the bottom for Formal Training and Special Skills like speaking a foreign language. You can use my **Professional Performance Resume Template** to create your own resume in the **Book Bonus Encore Page (http://jessicaneighbor.com/book-bonuses)**.

If you are younger and don't have many performance credits, be sure to write down all school and community shows you have participated in since you started out. Be sure to write out your training, in-school choirs and drama classes, as they count for a younger performer. As you gain more experience, you will graduate your resume to reflect your more current shows. It's exciting to list out all of the productions you have performed in, the list will continue to grow, the longer you perform!

My Industry Insider tip on Resumes: Don't put down a special skill on your resume unless you are really skilled at it! I once wrote that I could surf on my acting resume because I had managed to stand up for one wave in San Diego with my surfer cousin, and although I was never up for a surfer role, my acting friends teased me incessantly for writing that "special skill" in my resume.

I also once "expanded" a scene I did in an acting class and implied that I was in the full length play version on my resume. This did land me in the hot seat. At an audition, the Director asked me more about that production, he said it was one of his favorite plays, and I had to confess that I was only in a scene. I was caught in a lie which was embarrassing and just ethically wrong.

Your Headshot: Headshots are a photograph that represents you as a performer. It's smart to invest in a professional headshot and now, online, you can post multiple headshots. The goal for your headshot is to make it look like you on a good day.

Headshots can be tricky for rising stars because you are

growing and changing rapidly and your photos of yourself are as well. I suggest finding a headshot photographer who takes professional photos, but can also capture the "younger" and "older" part of your look, so that you have some wiggle room before you have to redo your photos. School pictures are generally not acceptable. The price can vary widely for headshots, when just starting out go for a reasonable headshot rate that you can afford. If you hire a professional photographer, read their reviews and ask for samples before you hire them.

My Industry Insider tip on headshots: You want to walk into the room and have your headshot reflect the true you. Your eyes are the most important feature in your headshot. Don't wear too much makeup or do your hair differently from normal, be yourself.

Your Showreel: A Showreel is video samples of your performances for potential casting agents. With a simple recorder, you can make a showreel to showcase your talents. Many Casting Agents require a show reel as part of your portfolio. Include a reel of live video recordings for each section of your skills: acting, singing, and dancing. This is like a live resume that shows a sampling of what you can do.

Choose short, varying pieces that highlight your dynamic range as a performer. Display 30-60 seconds of each piece, you can fade in and out different samples, and make sure to title and give credit for each piece in your reel. Young performer reels should run around 3 minutes in total length. You can make yours at home with a decent recorder and a neutral backdrop. Record yourself from the waste up and wear neutral clothing. Samples from live performances are also great to include if the quality is decent. You can use an editing App or hire an editor to put your video samples all together.

Your Vocal Demo: If you are a vocalist, you may also need to include a vocal recording of samples of your singing. This is called your vocal demo, a term that is short for your vocal demonstration. A vocal demo is usually for vocalists breaking into the music industry. You will want to choose 3-4 songs, and about 30-45 seconds of each, and choose dynamic styles to showcase your vocal range and talent. You can make a very inexpensive demo at home with a decent microphone and a home recording program. Or you can hire a recording engineer with a studio to record for you.

Your Sheet Music: If you are auditioning for vocals or musical theatre, you will often need to provide sheet music for each of your audition songs. Sheet music is the written composition of your audition song. It's important for a vocalist to have a good understanding of their sheet music. You want to learn the basic fundamentals of written music to understand your sheet music, how to read the melody, how to choose and identify the music key, and with a little training, you can attain these skills.

My Industry Insider Advice on Sheet Music: You will be expected to count in your accompanist (pianist) for your audition. Make sure you understand the tempo speed you want to sing your song, and you should practice your count-in with your voice or audition coach. Remember that a slower ballad usually requires a slow count of four, while a faster tempo will need an eight beat count-in.

I always have my performers clearly mark the start and end point, and any tempo or dynamic directions on their sheet music in the upper left hand corner of the first page. They practice communicating these directions with the accompanist when they meet them in a succinct way, usually right before their audition. The clearer you mark your sheet music, the better your accompanist can play for you!

Remember that the accompanist's job is to accompany you, and that means that you are leading the way for them. Very often, newer vocalists will make the mistake of following the accompanist when it is really the singer that should lead the way. You are the singer, and thus the leader of your song. Sing it as you have rehearsed it and the accompanist will follow your lead. There is a wide range of accompanist talent, regardless of how good or not good they are, you should be able to sing your song well from start to finish!

How to find sheet music: You can find sheet music online and download individual sheet music or purchase anthologies. I recommend the interactive music sheet downloads because they will play back your sheet music, so you can practice and you can change your vocal key.

YOUR AUDITION MATERIAL CHECKLIST:

As you get closer to your audition, you'll want to have your portfolio prepared and presentable. Don't wait until the last minute to assemble your audition portfolio. Do a check list at least a week before, to make sure that you have all your materials.

1. **Your Song's Sheet Music:** Make sure that you have enough copies of your printed out sheet music for the judges, pianist, and always keep a master copy for yourself! Tape your sheet music together so that the judges and/or the pianist can display it for themselves easily. If it's a long song, over 5 pages, then give them two sets of taped music that they will easily switch during the song. **Do not staple the sheet music!** If your vocal audition does not require sheet music and you are singing a cappella, then make sure you know the starting note for your song. Use a pitch pipe or piano app to locate your starting note.

2. **Your Headshot/Resume:** Make sure that you have enough copies of your current headshot and resume and that your resume is up to date. Have a portfolio holder to keep all of your materials looking perfect and professional.

3. **Your Audition Outfit:** Unless there are specific require-ments, you should wear something neutral for your audition day. I like to tell my younger clients that the audition day is like picture day at school. You want to look like yourself, on your best day. If you are an adult, dress like you would for a lunch date with a friend, nothing too formal. Do not do something dramatically different to your hair, outfit or makeup from what you usually look like. Your headshot should match what you look like currently. Practice rehearsing in your outfit to make sure that you feel comfortable.

4. **Your self-care audition kit:** I created this concept because as a young performer, I never brought much of what I needed to take care of myself at my audition. I was so focused on mastering my material and getting my audition portfolio organized, that I forgot to take care of myself. As I started coaching performers for auditions, I wanted to make sure that they took care of themselves with their own self-care audition kit. It's a good practice to help you stay calm, healthy, and happy.

Pack your goodies for your audition, so that you can take care of yourself. A real pro always has their essentials close at hand.

You can individualize your kit, but a good **self-care audition kit** should include:

1. A bottle of water

2. Healthy snacks that won't irritate your voice.

3. A book to read while waiting.

4. Your music player with headphones with a positive mindset playlist.

5. Photos of your loved ones that make you feel good.

6. Breath mints.

7. A good luck charm.

8. Love notes from friends and family to keep up your spirits.

Meryl Streep's good luck charm is a small note in her shoe, be creative about what will work for you!

1. Make sure you have your full audition portfolio and read over each item described to understand what they are and why they are important.

2. Use my **audition portfolio checklist in this chapter** to confirm that you have everything you need.

3. **Lights, Camera, Action:** Fill out your **Easy Professional Resume Template** in The **Book Bonus Encore Page (http:// jessicaneighbor.com/book-bonuses)**.

4. Don't forget to pack yourself a **self-care audition kit**. Taking care of yourself is so important for your audition success.

CHAPTER 8:

Build Your
Dream Support Team

E very performer needs a support team in their performance journey. You need to know who can help you in different areas of your performance needs, like who can get you to rehearsals, who can teach you, who can cheer you on, and with whom you can share your hopes and fears.

Here are the different cast members for your life's play starring YOU. Think about which people in your life can work for these roles? Don't be afraid to ask for help, no rising star gets there alone! Your Dream Team supports different parts of your performance life. Here are their roles:

1. **Your Supporting Cast**

2. **Your Fan Club**

3. **Your Coach**

4. **Your Confidant/BFF**

1. **Your Supporting Cast:** These are the people or person who help you with the practical things in your performance life like driving you to practice, signing you up for auditions, helping email and call about lessons and rehearsal times,

and helping you financially. This cast member will be important to help keep you on track with your guidelines and deadlines. This person should be highly organized and responsible.

My Supporting Cast is: _____

2. **Your Fan Club:** These are your friends and family who can cheer you on when you are up or down. They go to your shows, they encourage you to go for it, they are positive for you! These people should care about you, be positive, and be reliable to show up for you.

My Fan Club is: _____

3. **Your Coach:** Your Coach is that person with performance experience who can teach you. An audition coach, voice coach, drama teacher, or mentor are all great options for this important role. Trust this mentor to give you constructive criticism and pointers to help you grow as a performer. They should help you prepare your acting and singing for your auditions and give you feedback about your performances.

My Coach is: _____

4. **Your Confidant/BFF:** This person is your trusted friend with whom you can share your feelings. You can talk through your fears and hopes and they will support you emotionally. This person could be a close friend, relative, or counselor who is comfortable talking about feelings and can give you unconditional love when you need it.

My Confidant/BFF is: _____

All of these categories are important. Some people may fill more than one role, but notice that you don't want to rely on just one person for all of these roles, it's too many hats for them to wear! Find the people who are naturally good at these things and be sure to help them as well, and thank them along the way. Don't forget to thank them in your Oscar speech some day!

CHAPTER 8 WRAP-UP:

1. Remember to build your team so that you have the support you need!

2. No performer makes it alone.

3. Use the spaces provided to write out your dream team members.

CHAPTER 9:

The Judges- What to Know and How to Talk to Them

BEING JUDGED:

It's so natural for performers to feel sensitive about the judges at their audition, after all, the Judge's job is to judge you. Remember that they are there to find the best talent (that's you) for this role or production. They are under pressure too, just like you, to choose the right performers and to make good choices for the other people running the show. A casting director might have 500 people try out for one role, that's a lot of performers to watch, interview, evaluate, and then choose from and hope they make the right decision. So if you think about it, judges are under a lot of pressure too!

Let's flip the script for a moment. If you were a judge, what would you love to see from a performer at an audition? Let's list some qualities you would be looking for in a performer. You would want them to be...

- Talented
- Friendly
- Easy to work with

- Responsible
- Confident
- Prepared
- Positive
- Respectful
- Professional
- Fun

Notice that the "talent" is just one of the qualities. You would want someone who came into the audition room who felt nice, open, easy to talk with, and talented too. Notice that your talent is important but so is your interaction with the judges "off script" before and after your audition. As a judge, you are not only looking for talent, you are also looking for someone who would be easy to work with. If a performer seems really nervous, you may wonder if they can handle the pressure of the actual show. As a judge, you would wonder, "If they are this nervous at the audition in front of me, how will they handle a crowd of five thousand, or a camera crew, or a music producer?"

You want to make the judge's job easy. You do this by simply being yourself, a normal, down to earth human being. You have great value, because you are the talent. It does not feel that way from the waiting room full of your competitors, but if you can show them that you are skilled and easy to talk with, you will make a great impression.

Here are some specific pointers, so you know how to talk with the judges. Remember, they are just people like you. Many of them started out as performers too. They understand that auditions are stressful. They know you may feel nervous. They want you to be good. Make their job easy by showing them that you have got what it takes, here's how:

How to introduce yourself and talk with the judges

1. **Your Entrance:** Enter the audition room with your head held high. Remember that the judges are getting to know you from the instant you step through that door until the time

you leave the room. Be friendly and positive. They may engage you in a little small talk at first, "Hello, where are you from? What school do you go to?" or they may say nothing at all and wait for you to begin your piece. Be prepared for either situation, it does not mean they dislike you. If they do not ask you questions, be ready for your introduction, what we call in the performance industry "Your slate"

2. **Your Slate:** Your slate is your introduction right before your audition piece. In your slate you will say:

"Hello, my name is (your name) "_____" and I will be performing the song (song title)" _____" by (song composer)"_____".

If this is a TV or film audition, you will also say your age after your name. If this is a musical theater audition, you will say the name of the play after the song composer. If this is a monologue, you will say your character and the title and author of the play.

Practice your slate! This seems like a simple enough introduction, but the pressure is on and the last thing you want to do is mess up your introduction. Say it in a natural way with energy and engage with your eyes. Look at the judges, this is the right time to make direct eye contact with them. After your introduction, you will start your audition piece.

Practice your slate every time before you practice your audition song from here on!

The Judge Corner: A few key things to remember about the judges:

1. They want you to be good! These judges are trained to look for talented performers. They are rooting for you. They may or may not "seem" friendly, but remember that they may audition over 100 people at a time and they are on a tight schedule. Don't let their facial expression or demeanor throw you off your game, they really want you to be fantastic!

2. Judges are people just like you. Although it may seem like they hold all the power, remember that it is their job to find good performers. Your job is to be that good performer. Judges and performers NEED each other. Plus, most judges used to be performers themselves, so they understand your situation.

3. Make the judges feel comfortable. I have judged vocal competitions and cast plays before, and I'm always so relieved when a nice, normal, and positive performer walks through that door. Don't get too close to them, it's their job to observe you. Don't stare them down your entire audition. DO act natural and be positive even though you may feel nervous. They are judging you on your talent and thinking about what kind of a person you are to work with. They want to know if you are friendly, reliable, and a team player. Put on your best self the entire time you are in front of the judges!

My Industry Insider Advice on Judges: Research Your Judges. You may have no idea who you will be auditioning for, but if you can find out, do your research. If you can find out about the judge, you will have an advantage. You can do a simple Google search, or look at their Linkedin profile, to get a general sense about them. You can always send in an email or call about material preferences ahead of time. Ask also about their no-go lists: material they do NOT want to hear.

Your Possible First Interview You may have a brief interview at your first round audition if time permits and if they want to know more about you. Very often your answers are not as important as the way you answer as I'll explain.

At my Audition Skills Summer Program Intensive, I train teen performers in audition skills, and I have mock auditions with my student performers, so that they can practice their interviews. Remember, they may not ask you any questions and still accept, hire you, or call you back for another audition.

One of the most common mistakes that my students made at my audition program was to "Kill their interview". For example, I asked one performer a simple practice question, "What's your favorite dessert?" as a way to get to know her more, and she answered, "I don't like dessert". She just killed her interview. A better answer would be to say, "Oh, what's my favorite dessert? Wow, I love so many, I did just have Tiramisu at an Italian Restaurant for the first time and I loved it".

Do you see how the second answer is more inviting to continue the interview, how it breathes life into the conversation? The judge does not care WHAT your favorite dessert actually is, they care about how you are communicating with them. Are you engaging, are you authentic, are you answering with energy?

My student, who really did not like dessert, figured out a better answer which was to say, "Oh, I actually don't like desserts but I could eat dried seaweed all day long". This is a great answer as well because she shared something true about herself, a unique love of seaweed, that the judges are sure to remember. The point of the brief interview is to get just a "taste" of what you are like, be it salty or sweet, your goal is to leave them wanting MORE.

Here are some general audition interview questions that you should prepare just in case they ask you:

AUDITION INTERVIEW QUESTIONS

1. Why do you want to be in this production or program?
2. Why do you like to perform?
3. Who is your favorite singer? Actor? Performer?
4. What is your favorite musical? Movie? Book? Why?
5. Where do you go to school and what's your favorite subject at school?
6. What else do you have for us?

My Industry Insider Interview Tip: This last question #6, "What else do you have for us?" is a great one to be asked! This means that they want to hear more from you. This is where your plan B material comes in. Remember the actress friend of mine in Los

Angeles who had to perform all those monologues for an audition even though initially they only asked for one? It's a good thing she had those monologues rehearsed, she got in. Many of my performers have been asked to perform another piece which is why I always have them prepare plan B material just in case. Plan C and plan D material is great to have ready too.

CHAPTER 9 WRAP-UP:

1. **Remember that judges are under pressure too**. Try to put yourself in their shoes.

2. **Practice your slate and how you enter the room**- this is your very important first impression.

3. **Put the judges at ease** by being prepared, pleasant, and respectful of their space.

4. **Lights, Camera, Action: Practice your possible interview questions in this chapter**. Remember that staying positive is best.

5. **Have your plan b material ready** if they ask you for more!

CHAPTER 10:

How to prepare for different types of auditions

Schedule out your practice time in advance: The best way to schedule out your home practice to prepare for your audition is to look at your audition date and work backwards from there. Some auditions are posted months in advance affording you a luxurious amount of time to practice for it. Others may be last minute, like tomorrow, and you will have just a few hours to prepare. Here are my suggestions for short-term and long-term audition dates.

Have your audition material repertoire ready for action: The most important thing to prepare for your audition, short notice or long term, is to know your regular audition repertoire. If you are a musical theatre performer, this means that you have a solid group of songs and monologues in your wheelhouse that you can perform in a pinch. Your audition repertoire you will develop over time, but it's important for even a new performer to get a few audition staples prepared, so that when opportunity knocks, you are ready to answer.

A TRIPLE THREAT PERFORMER SHOULD HAVE THE FOLLOWING AUDITION REPERTOIRE READY:

1. A ballad/slow song with sheet music
2. An uptempo/fast song with sheet music
3. A comedic monologue from a published production
4. A dramatic monologue from a published production
5. One classical monologue from a published production

IS YOUR MATERIAL WORKING FOR YOU?

You want to make sure that you are choosing the right repertoire for yourself. If you are getting consistently declined at auditions, it's probably your choice of repertoire. One of my main jobs as an audition coach is to assess if your repertoire is truly your strongest choice for your particular talent.

SHORT NOTICE AUDITION PREPARATION:

If you have a short notice audition, you will be glad that you have some repertoire already learned. If you have only short notice for your audition and you can choose your piece, do not try to learn a new piece unless it's required for the audition. Use your repertoire. The more you use your regular material, the better you'll get at them.

If you have to learn a new required piece for a short notice audition, remember that you want to keep your expectations realistic. If you have just a few days to memorize a new piece, try to gain the main essence of the piece rather than every detail. You are giving them your "rough sketch" of the character or song, you want to memorize and prepare enough so that what you show the judges, leaves them wanting more.

A short notice audition is not the time to try to "master" your new material. This is the time to go with your instincts and your first impressions about the character or song. Remember, you are giving them a sample of this role at the beginning of the production, not the final product with you in full costume and fully rehearsed- that will come once you get in! Your main objective is to think about what you need to do to GET IN, don't overwhelm yourself with all of the details for short-notice auditions.

Long Notice Audition Preparation:

If you have a longer term audition and you know your audition date months in advance, then you have more options about how to practice. This is a good opportunity to add a new piece to your repertoire that makes sense for your particular audition. Say you are going out for a musical comedy, but the audition guidelines instruct you to not sing a song from the musical, then you may want to refresh your song repertoire or expand it with a new comedic musical theatre audition piece.

There will be higher expectations for a longer term audition, say for a College Program or an Agent, because you are presenting your best prepared work and had plenty of time to do so.

Never make excuses to the judges about why you are not fully prepared for your long-term audition. If you realize too late that you did not practice enough, then that is your burden to know about, not the judges. Make the most of what you have prepared, do not apologize for it.

Think like a Chef

A good comparison to preparing for an audition without feeling fully prepared is thinking like a chef. What if you were preparing a meal, but you were missing a few of your regular ingredients and it was too late to get them. You improvise with what you have in your kitchen and it winds up tasting delicious, different from your usual recipe, but delicious. Would you serve your food and tell your guests that the meal they are about to eat is not good enough? No! You serve it with a smile and hope that they like it. We can't ultimately control if it will be to their taste, but we can absolutely control how we serve it with confidence.

TRAIN LIKE AN ATHLETE

Once you have worked backwards from your audition date, you'll know what's realistic for your practice schedule. Treat your audition like a marathon, you want to create a consistent training schedule for yourself. Get into a regular routine of practicing your audition material, you may want to schedule it into your daily schedule. I suggest that performers practice 5 days per week and give themselves two days off. Shorter and more consistent practice is always better than only doing one or two longer practices per week. You can refer to my practice tips from chapter 6 for more specific practice advice.

Write out your practice schedule and hold yourself accountable to it. Have your "Practical Team" give you check-ins to make sure you are staying on track. Try to get it into your daily routine.

Cold Reading Auditions: A cold reading is where you are handed a script, or a side, and asked to read it there on the spot. Sometimes, you'll have a few minutes to look it over, sometimes you'll be reading it completely cold for the first time in your life. Cold Readings can be intimidating but don't let them be, use your acting improvisation skills to go with your first choice for the character. If there is a reader, play off of their dialogue. I recommend that all performers do acting improvisation to think on your feet. Your improv skills will help you at cold readings. Enjoy your spontaneous delivery, it's low pressure because you just got the script. Have fun with cold readings!

Skype/Sent in Reel: More and more auditions are being held using video recordings. Sometimes these auditions are live, sometimes they are pre-recorded and sent in for an audition.

For live video auditions, treat it like you are in the same room as the judges with these important adjustments:

1. Make sure that your lighting is good. Natural light looks great or be sure to be well lit inside.

2. Have a neutral background for your video so they can focus on you.

3. Record from your waist or shoulders up, unless otherwise requested.

4. Check all of your computer & camera connections before your video audition.

5. Make sure that you are animated. Video can flatten and dull our performances, keep your energy up and try not to watch yourself as you perform your audition piece.

I did video audition coaching for a very talented vocalist who lived in Barcelona, Spain. She was applying for a competitive vocal program here in the states and she had to prepare a song and interview for her Skype Audition. When I first started working with her, I realized that she was very talented but that she appeared stiff and awkward on the video. We worked on ways to help her relax and get more used to performing to her computer screen.

After some intense coaching sessions, she grew relaxed and more natural when she sang her audition song.

All of her video audition coaching practice helped her get used to the format and she wound up being one of the few vocalists admitted into the vocal academic program! She will move from Spain to sunny California to pursue her performance dreams.

Video Recordings: If you have a performance agent, you will be expected to record your audition materials multiple times because they want to see your most current material that reflects your true age. This means you may sing the same song for multiple auditions. Treat this like a great chance to improve your audition song each time. Use a consistent background for your recordings and have a "recording set up" at your home. Practice your slate for each new audition and keep yourself animated for your slate and performance.

Otherwise, use my same audition training method in this book for your audition success, either at a live audition or a recorded/ Skype audition.

CHAPTER 10 WRAP-UP:

1. **Schedule your practice routine** for your audition day working back from the date to today. Schedule your practice plan and follow through! Have your support team check-in to make sure you are staying on track.

2. **Have your "go to" audition repertoire ready** for your auditions.

3. Understand the **different strategies** for short and long-term auditions.

4. **Video Auditions:** Be ready for the growing trend of auditioning through live or recorded video.

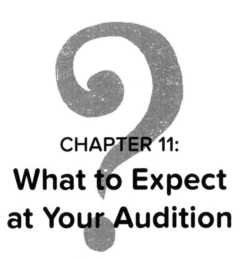

CHAPTER 11:

What to Expect
at Your Audition

- Arriving to your audition & checking in

- The Waiting Room

- The Audition

- After Your Audition

t's your big day! You have worked so hard to get here. In this section, we'll go over the typical scenario on your audition day with the reality that not every audition is the same. Remind yourself of what you have control over and what you do not. You can control how well you know your material, how prepared you are and your positive mindset. What you cannot control is the audition setting, the judges mood, the traffic that morning, and all of the other life events that are out of our control.

This section is a description of each step of your typical audition day to give you an idea of what to expect so that you can feel calm and centered.

1. **Arriving and checking in at your audition:** Usually there will be a check in station where you register for your audition. Be polite and respectful, your audition has just

started! This person registering you may very well be the judges' assistant and their opinion matters too. Have your materials ready, they will ask you to turn them in or hold onto them for the audition room. Make sure to confirm your audition time, where you should wait, and ask about the restroom. DO NOT ask about parking, if you can go and get coffee and come back, or if they can move up your audition time- Be professional!

In some auditions, there may not be a person to register with, so confirm with other performers that you are at the right place and wait for your call.

2. **The Waiting Room:** The waiting room may be a typical room, or a hallway, or a large lobby depending on your audition setting. This can be the most challenging time before your audition! This is where our mind can start to wander and our worry worms and inner hecklers can flare up. Find a place to get comfortable and use your self-care kit to help keep you focused and calm.

In the waiting room you can play your positive music playlist, low enough volume so that you can hear your name called. You can repeat your mantra or create your positive audition image outcome in your mind. Practice your deep breathing. Do not start doubting your material and cramming in a last minute practice. There is nothing useful at this stage about practicing. You are already fully prepared. Your job is to stay calm and focused.

Some performers enjoy talking with others to calm their nerves. If you do this, make sure to keep your conversation light and positive. If someone else seems too nervous or negative, politely excuse yourself. Do not act unprofessional in the waiting room. Now is not the time to make loud phone calls or start doing a dance routine. You are on call. They may call you in for your audition at any time now. Be ready and be set to go! Watch my **video** about feeling confident in the waiting room in **The Book Bonus Encore Page (http://jessicaneighbor.com/book-bonuses)**

3. **Your audition!** I wish I could tell you exactly how it will go, but this is game time and anything can happen. Just like an

athlete, you know your moves, you know your play, now it's time to go for it! Remember that the minute you enter the room, you are auditioning.

Typically you will say hello and wait to see if the judges ask you any questions. Remember to keep your answers short and sweet. It's "small talk" so that they can get a feel for you. They may ask, "How are you today?" or "Where are you from?" Give a nice answer, but they don't want your life story. They are checking you out, stay true to yourself.

PRACTICE THESE POSSIBLE JUDGE QUESTIONS:

"How are you today?"

"Where do you live?"

"Where do you go to school?"

"What do you like to do with your friends outside of school?"

"Why do you like to sing?"

"Why are you interested in our program/production?"

Don't memorize your answers but have a basic idea of how you will respond. This may sound harsh, but they don't really care about the specific answer. They care about your personality and how comfortable you are talking with them. They are thinking about what you are like as a person and what you will be like to work with in their program or production. They are checking if you are engaging, do you make eye contact, do you have a point of view? Don't worry about being perfect, just try to be perfectly you.

If the judges do not make small talk with you, don't worry, they just may be short on time. I have done auditions where the judges barely looked at me and I wound up getting in. If they tell you to begin, be prepared to go right into your prepared audition.

REMEMBER YOUR AUDITION PRESENTATION ORDER:

1. Hand your audition materials to the judges and pianist if applicable.

2. Say your Slate.

3. Perform your Audition Piece.

4. Be ready for follow up questions or further directions from judges.

5. Thank the judges and exit with your head held high.

AFTER YOUR AUDITION

After you perform your song or monologue, you are not done! You are still in the audition. The judges may say thank you, but they may also give you a direction. "Could you sing that again? Do you have anything else?" Be ready with your plan B material in this event! Remember, If they ask you to do something different, that's great! That means that they are interested and want to see more of you. Try not to take their feedback in a negative way.

Once it is clear that you are done with your audition, make sure to take a moment to thank each of the judges with direct eye contact Even if they cut you off after 10 seconds, always thank them and assume the best. Your job is to be gracious. Before you leave, smile and say thank you, and walk out the door with your head held high.

An important side note about your integrity and safety at auditions: Most judges are professionals but some judges may try to abuse their power. Never do anything in an audition that you feel crosses the line of decency. Keep your self-respect and make sure that they are respectful to you. Never go to an audition in an isolated location where you are the only performer. You are a professional and the judges should always be professional too! Report any strange audition to the authorities.

Now it's time for your reward and self- evaluation: Give yourself a small reward after each audition. Auditions are not easy, you have really applied yourself and put yourself out there. After your audition, we usually have a million questions running through our heads. Give yourself a little time to process your audition experience with a friend or write it down and log it in your journal. We learn from every audition experience, that's what makes us get better.

Your reward: Go for a walk, have a yummy treat, go exercise, do something fun for yourself to reward yourself after putting yourself out there. Do not get down on yourself or beat yourself up if you made a mistake. Remember, we learn from each experience and get better that way. I made every mistake in the book! Be your own best friend and support team. You just did a brave thing that most people would never dare do! Do you know that most people would rather jump out of an airplane and parachute than speak in public? Give yourself a big pat on the back, you deserve it!

CHAPTER 11 WRAP-UP:

1. **Know the steps of your audition day:** Checking in, the waiting room, your audition, and your exit.

2. **Know the order of your typical audition:** Your entrance, slate, audition material, possible interview, thank the judges, and exit.

3. **Lights, Camera, Action:** Prepare for the waiting room with my **"Waiting Room" video in the Book Bonus Encore Page (http://jessicaneighbor.com/book-bonuses)**

4. **Reward yourself** after your audition. You deserve it!

CHAPTER 12:
Positive Mindset Training for Your Audition Day

We want to plan out your positive mindset for your actual audition day, so that you will feel your most relaxed, positive, and excited. Here is my positive coaching strategy for the week before, the day before, and your actual audition day. I have each of my performers use this strategy and their feedback has been overwhelmingly positive!

1. **Write out your daily mantra-** A mantra is a repeated phrase that we tell ourselves. What we tell ourselves leading up to our audition has a great impact on our performance. If we keep reminding ourselves that we are not prepared or not good enough, we may believe those things! Here are three of my performer's chosen mantras:

    "I got this!"

    "Yes, I can!"

    "How will I know unless I try"

    Remind yourself of this comforting quote,

    "If not you, then who? If not now, then when?

Find a comforting phrase or quote that makes you feel good. Say it to yourself every day this week. This is really the time to believe in yourself. If you don't believe in yourself, then who will?

2. **Plan out your week before your audition to take care of yourself:** Avoid stress the week before your audition. You have a full life with responsibilities, try to pace yourself the week leading up to your audition. You are in training. Eat right, drink plenty of water, and get enough sleep. You can write out your calendar week. Anticipate your deadlines or assignments. Avoid drama. Take care of yourself. Say your daily mantra.

3. **Plan out your day before your audition to take care of yourself:** Try to make the night before your audition a restful night. Do comforting things so that you feel good and are well rested for your big day.

4. **The day of your audition**- Try to warm up at least two hours before your audition. Do your physical and vocal exercises early in the day. Eat a healthy meal so you have sufficient fuel for your audition- you need energy.

    Plan your trip to the audition site and give yourself extra time to park, walk, and arrive early and calm. You will probably feel nervous. Don't let your nerves make you do things like get lost, run late, or get overwhelmed. You are in training, you can handle this. You want this audition, you deserve this audition, you have worked hard for this audition. Now, go in there and give it your best shot. Break a leg, not your spirit.

HERE ARE CENTERING EXERCISES TO DO RIGHT BEFORE YOUR AUDITION:

1. **Do Calm Breathing Exercises:** Breathe in for 4 slow counts, breathe out for 4 slow counts. Fill up your whole torso with breath, so you are using your diaphragm and getting the most deep breath possible, this will help calm you.

2. **Envision your positive outcome:** Close your eyes, find a peaceful place to sit, and imagine the positive audition scenario that you wrote out in your "Positive Audition Outcome Scenario" writing exercise.

3. **Keep your inner-heckler and worry worm in check**, they are not welcome nor needed here at your audition.

4. **Do stretches, yoga, or a spontaneous dance party**: If it's appropriate, find a place to stretch, move, or even "shake out" your jitters with some dancing. I often have my performers do jumping jacks or dance right before their audition to stay loose and relaxed.

5. **Do Squeeze/Release Body Isolations**

6. **Read your love notes** from your "fan club".

Here are centering exercises to do once you are IN the audition room:

If you enter the audition and your nerves spike up, what I like to call a "Nervous Creeper Wave", then there are still strategies to do in that moment to calm yourself down. Some of the things you do in private, like stretching and meditating, would not be appropriate in front of the judges.

1. You can still take a moment to take deep breaths.

2. You can smile and feel the positive shift that a smile will bring.

3. You can ground your feet and hands if you start to feel shaky using my "busy body" video tutorials.

4. You can say your mantra in your head to yourself.

5. You can give yourself the green light to just go for it!

Watch my Audition Day Positive Mindset Video for more help in the Book Bonus Encore Page (http://jessicaneighbor. com/book-bonuses).

CHAPTER 12 WRAP-UP:

1. **Write out your mantra and plan for your positive mindset audition day.** This way you give yourself a road map!

2. **Choose your pre-audition room centering exercises** from the list in this chapter. Choose the ones that feel good to you.

3. **Choose your in-audition room calming exercises** from the list in this chapter in case you experience a "nervous creeper wave".

4. **Lights, Camera, Audition:** Watch my **Audition Day Positive Mindset Video** in The **Book Bonus Encore Page (http:// jessicaneighbor.com/book-bonuses)**

CHAPTER 13:

What to Expect
After Your Audition

- The Results
- Self-Review
- Personal Rewards and Positive Benefits of Auditioning

THE RESULTS

You went in there and you did your best. Now you have to wait for your results. Did you get the part? Did you get rejected? Did you get a callback? Each of these results will likely happen to you during your performance journey. Every performer has been rejected and accepted. Let's change the thinking from "I did not get it" to "I did not get it yet".

A huge part of being a performer is learning to play the audition game and not taking the audition results too personally. Yes, it stinks when we are left out. However, don't let that discourage you. Take notes for your next audition, persistence pays off, and know that your time will come if you keep at it. Auditioning is like a muscle that we develop over time. You have the needed skills, now it's time to use your audition skills regularly and repeatedly to have success.

Remember, if you did your best at your audition, that's all you can do. That is the definition of success!

Self-Review: In my private coaching, I always schedule up a follow-up session after a performer's audition. This way we can talk over and review how their audition went. No matter what the outcome, we learn and grow from each audition experience.

> *"Success takes communication, collaboration, and sometimes failure"*
>
> *-Jessica Alba, Actor*

It's important to first let yourself feel the different emotions right after your audition. You may feel pleased, or frustrated with how you did. You may feel very proud or very embarrassed. Often, you will feel a combination of these emotions, so allow yourself to process all of these feelings after you put yourself out there to be judged.

In my coaching follow-up session, we sort through these different emotions to find which ones will help us and which feelings we need to move through and let go. I usually ask open ended questions to hear about the audition experience.

SOME OF THE KEY QUESTIONS TO ASK YOURSELF OR TALK OVER WITH SOMEONE ELSE ARE:

1. How did you feel about your audition?
2. What were you happy about in your audition?
3. What surprised you?
4. What do you wish could have gone differently? If you could do it again, would you change anything?
5. What was something you are proud about doing in your audition?

6. On a scale of 1-10, how good do you feel about your audition?

7. How will you feel if you get in?

8. How will you feel if you do not get in? What will you do to take care of yourself so you don't get too discouraged? Remember, this is not a "no forever", just a "not now".

9. What did you learn from this audition experience for next time?

10. How are you going to celebrate your bravery for doing this audition?

You can watch my video on "How to review your audition" in the Book Bonus Encore Section

THREE HELPFUL TIPS FOR YOUR SELF-REVIEW:

1. Do this review a day or two after your audition when your nerves have settled but your audition is still fresh in your memory. A great practice is to journal and write down your review so that you have a record of your audition experiences.

2. In my audition coaching follow-up session, I am always very clear to remind clients that we are not here to beat ourselves up about our auditions. We are here to review our audition, so that we grow and develop our "audition muscle".

3. It can be helpful to process your audition with a trusted person, but make sure that you record your own experience for yourself.

PERSONAL REWARDS AND POSITIVE BENEFITS OF AUDITIONING
REGARDLESS OF RESULTS

This can be a comforting section for more experienced performers and new performs alike because all of you must keep the focus on your journey and not the latest result or stop in the road. You may score a huge part or get a rejection notice, you may likely get both at some point, and multiple times over. There will be highs and lows in your performance career. The most important thing that you do is to stay in the game and not get discouraged.

From auditioning, you will gain these positive benefits that will help all aspects of your life.

FROM AUDITIONS YOU WILL LEARN...

1. How to take risks
2. How to follow through with a dream
3. How to present yourself to people in power with dignity and grace
4. How to let your light shine even under tremendous pressure
5. How to control your nerves
6. How to command a room with your physical presence
7. How to go for something, even if the odds are against you, and be brave
8. How to make new possibilities happen in your life
9. How to put yourself out there
10. How to meet new people in the industry

A final love note from Coach Jessica: Remind yourself time and time again leading up to your audition that all you can do is be yourself. You will put in your practice using my coaching preparation strategy, and your positive mindset training, so you have your "prepared-spontaneity" ready for whatever happens at your audition. What a challenge and what an accomplishment for you to follow through with this training! You will have many chances to practice and grow your audition skills. It's by doing them and having the audition skills know-how, that you are on your way. What a gift, what a fantastic opportunity to try and shine your brightest at each of your auditions. Keep shining, keep growing, and you will have an amazing life journey!

CHAPTER 13 WRAP-UP

1. **Remember that the results are important, but your process is the most important thing.**

2. **Lights, Camera, Action: Self-Review** and talk with someone you trust about your experience. Record it for your future reference.

3. **Lights, Camera, Action:** Watch my **"Self-Review" Video** in the **Book Bonus Encore Page (http://jessicaneighbor. com/book-bonuses)**.

4. Congratulations, you have now completed your audition skills training method to help you reach your dream, one audition at a time!

CHAPTER 14:
Strategies for Parents of Rising Star Performers

This chapter is dedicated to you hard working parents of performers. I know how much you support your child. You schedule their enrichment classes, shuttle them across town to their long rehearsals, and then you applaud them wildly at their shows!

I'd like to coach you in this chapter on how you can play your optimal role to best support your performance child. You may need a little support in figuring out how to navigate this crazy performance industry! As a child performer myself, and a Mother of two young sons, I can relate to both sides. I often hear about your concerns for your child: Can they handle the rejection? Do they have what it takes? Is this performance career healthy for my child?

A lot of parents of performers can get a bad rap. "Stage Mom" and "Star Dad" are names that bring up an often negative image of a pushy parent who thinks their child is better than everyone else. I have to say that from my experience of working with these parents over the past twenty years, this can't be further from the truth. These parents embrace their child's performance passion. So why can being a performance parent, a term I much prefer, sometimes feel confusing and frustrating?

Often your parent role is not clear, especially how to help your own child navigate their performance ups and downs. One minute they may cry to you and seek comfort about getting rejected from an audition, and the next day they suddenly want no feedback about their next audition. Talk about a 180 degree turn! Perhaps your child is making some seemingly obvious poor choices in their performance that you would simply like to point out. I will explain why you must try not to take on the role of a coach or director. Your child needs a team and you are their team leader, whether they want to always fully admit it or not. Let's define your role clearly and use tried and true strategies to support your performance child so you can fully enjoy the journey together.

MY OWN POSITIVE PERFORMANCE PARENTING WAKE UP CALL:

When my son, Finn, enrolled in a local soccer league at age 6, I was required to attend a positive parent training night. I scoffed at the idea that I even needed to go. I was fine, as if I could ever be a crazy soccer Mom who screamed from the sidelines. What I did not realize was at the first few games, before this orientation, I unconsciously started coaching Finn from the bleachers and I was crossing the healthy boundaries of positive parenting.

I had played a few years of soccer myself in elementary and junior high in a local league, and I always felt mediocre at best. My best friend was the team star player who would eventually get a full college soccer scholarship at an Ivy League School. We were competitive and I quickly realized that I did not have the same natural athletic abilities. It was not until I tried out for my middle school play and got the lead role that I found my calling and chance. I lost my motivation in soccer when I realized I was not "the best". I did not want my son to go through that same experience. I wanted my son to go for soccer and believe in himself. I did not want him to feel the same bitter-sweet emotions that I felt from playing soccer. I subconsciously wanted him to be a better and stronger version of myself.

This feeling manifested itself in my sideline comments, "Keep your eye on the ball!", and "Get in there, Finn!" I was being positive, right? I was not screaming insults at him or being mean. I was cheering him on, and trying to help him to see the obvious, "You have a shot, take it, take it!"

So I was quite surprised at the positive parenting orientation when I realized that I was doing a subtler version of negative parenting. Some huge takeaways from that training apply precisely to performance parents as well. **Here are the six strategies to play a positive role for your child:**

STRATEGY 1: DON'T COACH YOUR OWN CHILD.

This lesson has an obvious and more subtle practice. The obvious lesson is to not direct your own child's performances and rehearsals, leave coaching to the director or coach involved. The reason is because your main job is to be the audience for your child, not the expert. They want you to witness and support their performance life- not control it!

The more subtle part is that you want to watch what you say closely, even when your child asks for your feedback. They are already super sensitive around you, we must be very mindful about what we say to them and think clearly about our own motives.

I want to share a tutorial video about what to say to your child after you watch them in a performance. How do you compliment them, what do they need from you? Often parents say the wrong thing without having a clue that they just insulted their child! **Watch my video, "What to say to your child after their performance", in the Book Bonus Encore Page (http://jessicaneighbor.com/ book-bonuses)**

STRATEGY 2: PERFORMANCE IS A PROCESS, NOT A PRODUCT.

Remember that your performance child is developing their talent and the training process is slow. They may take singing lessons, for instance, and still sound less than perfect. Vocal and dramatic development takes time and nothing can stunt it more than a parent saying something cruel to their child. Your child may be a rare protege, but most likely they have raw talent and really just love performing at first. I'll have parents confide in me, "I don't think my child can sing that well" or "Does he have what it takes- I'm not sure?" None of us are ever "sure", as a youth we do what we enjoy and if we truly love it, we will find a way to get better at it. Remember that even if your child is not destined for Broadway, their performance and audition skills of taking risks and being brave will last them their entire lifetime.

Your job is to support their performance process, regardless of their results. That means encouraging them to try out for shows, giving them access to training methods, and allowing them to have their own reactions to each of these tried experiences. A young performer is developing their talent as they are maturing, so let them enjoy their own talent "growing" process.

Strategy 3: Applaud- but not too loud!

Let me tell you a true story about a parent who was just a little too enthusiastic about her performance child. In my early twenties, I was a lead vocalist in musical theatre troupe that performed original Rock Operas in Los Angeles and San Francisco. In a San Francisco production, one of the funniest performers in our troupe had an overzealous Mom. We always knew when she was in the audience because she laughed the loudest, the longest, and she had a high pitch signature tone. What's wrong with this Mom, you may say? She just loved watching her son perform. Well, it drove her son, and the rest of us, a little bonkers because she was so distracting. Talk about upstaging from the audience. Of course, she meant well, and she loved her son dearly and supported his performance pursuits, she just came on a little too strong.

There are a lot of articles and research in parenting that discuss the issue of over-praising our children. The main concern with too much praise is that it starts to feel empty and insincere. Or worst yet, our children start to seek it out but it never feels fulfilling because they were overloaded with praise. I am a very vocal parent who cheers loudly from the soccer sidelines still, but I have to temper my enthusiasm so that I don't "steal my child's thunder". I also want to reward his effort, not just his wins. This is crucial for audition parents, especially because you know that there will be inevitable disappointments. We win some and we lose some, your main job is to keep them in the game- if they want to be there.

Strategy 4: Whose dream is it?

This may be the hardest lesson to learn as a parent and will take ongoing check-ins with yourself and your child: Whose dream is it to be a performer? There are some parents who had or have performance aspirations and recognize a similar talent in their children. So how do they support their child's journey without projecting their own old hopes and dreams on to them? Parents need to be open to the truth that your child's journey is going to be different from your own. Your child's performance goals may be different, as well as their taste and style of performing. Their performance dreams may also shift and fade, or grow in ways you never got to experience. Recognize that their journey is their own. You can't be there with them onstage or in that audition room. Show your support by being a constant and positive figure in their performances, but give them space to realize their own dreams.

Strategy 5: Give yourself a hand.

You are a parent doing the best you can, and we all know that parenting is a process that does not come with a script. If you are supporting your child in their performance endeavors, then you yourself deserve a round of applause. You recognize the value in the performing arts and even if you don't totally get it, you support it! The next generation is going to do things a bit differently, we may feel like we are falling behind the times or don't "get" the latest music or performance craze. That's OK! You have your own separate world and tastes, you can expose your child to some of your favorites too, as long as you don't force it on them or expect them to like it.

You may drive your young performer to voice lessons, or sign them up for drama camp, get them expensive headshots, or simply encourage them to go out for their school talent show. You are being present and positive in your child's life- that's amazing!

Keep the dialogue open with your performance child, listen more and talk less, try to be a sounding board for them.

There is a cultural bias against performance parents. Why is it that Serena William's Dad or Michael Phelp's Mom is applauded while so many stage parents are vilified when they are doing essentially the same things: taking your child to long and regular rehearsals, going to all of their shows, and supporting them through their ups and downs. I for one would like to commend your efforts! You are giving your child rich opportunities, not to mention the spotlight, and very often yours' is an underappreciated role. Well I say to you, Bravo! Job well done!

STRATEGY 6: TAKE CARE OF YOURSELF.

Make sure that you are taking care of yourself in this process. Especially around auditions and shows, a lot of your impulses to protect your child are going to flare up. Just recognize those natural tendencies and try not to run with them. Also notice that if your child is not applying themselves, say not practicing, that will be their own struggle to manage. You can provide the structure for practice, but it's up to your child to apply themselves.

In the beginning of my coaching, I like to sit down with a new family to talk about the ways we can work as a team for their performance child. Everyone needs to be doing their part. Your child has to do the work or else they will falter at some stage in their development. Nothing is harder than letting your child fail. Yet we know in performance that rejection is part of our reality. Why not start letting them struggle in small and healthy doses to gain the resilience they will need in the entertainment world.

Your child may have their sights set on a role or a program that you believe is out of their reach. Let them go for it, let them figure it out for themselves. You are not the casting director who says, "Thank You but we are going a different direction". You are not their agent who helps them to form their "performance type", you are not their director who tells them their cues, you are not their voice coach who asks them to "sing it again", you are their parent who provides access to these people and that access in itself is so valuable.

How to choose the best coach for your young performer

Many parents are not sure about the right age to start private vocal or audition coaching for their child. I am frequently asked the question, "Is my child ready for private coaching?" Some of it depends on the focus ability of the child, but I generally recommend starting private coaching between the ages of 10-12 years old.

I recommend group lessons for performers below 10 years old. I've seen how much more the very young performers learn from their peers in a group setting like in choirs, musical theater programs, or group lessons like my own small group vocal class, The Oakland Glee Program, (**www.jessicaneighbor.com**) for children ages 8-12. The program's emphasis should be about the fun and joy of music for very young performers.

A student who is ready for private coaching (www.jessicaneighbor.com) should be self-motivated. Doing their home practice should be a fun activity and not another chore to add to their long to-do list. Students should have clear goals that they work out with their Coach to help keep them stay motivated like preparing for an audition or a talent show.

There are many styles of Coaching out there, make sure that the coach is right for your child. Does your child enjoy the types of music that the Coach is an expert in teaching? Is their teaching method and personality style complimentary? I always schedule a preliminary lesson with my students to make sure that I am the right Coach for them.

You will also be working closely with this Coach so make sure they are a good fit for you too. Do they have clear teaching policies available for you? Are they transparent about billing and scheduling? Are they available for your questions and do they support you as well as your child?

Finally, your child should have input in the decision making as well. Talk over their introductory session with the coach to see how they felt about the experience. These Coaching sessions are for their personal growth and they will feel more invested when they are involved in the decision making process. Private Coaching is a wonderful and important step in the development of a young and motivated performer. Take the time to make the right choice for private coaching to ensure the most meaningful and effective experience for your child's performance development.

My own beloved Performance Parents

I am eternally grateful to my own parents for encouraging my performance process from age 5, when they were my first captive audience for my countless living room variety shows. They supported my performance shows throughout my school years in musicals and bands, and later my choice to major in Theatre at UCLA. I'm thankful that my parents travelled to LA and San Francisco and brought friends and family to attend my professional shows. They helped me to make my first music CD. They cheered me on throughout my high and low points, and they always made me feel good again by showing me that no matter what, I was always loved.

Now, as a Mother of two children myself, I realize all of the pitfalls that we parents have to navigate. I want my boys, Finn and Kaleo, to try new things, develop their talents, whether they wind up on the stage or not. Finn seems to love to sing and act, my younger son, Kaleo, likes to dance and play instruments, but hates the spotlight- so far. I want to provide all that I can for them and accept that when the lights in the audience go down, I must take my place in the crowd and love them from afar. I am now their supporting cast and they are their own rising star.

CHAPTER 14 WRAP-UP:

1. Embrace your title: **Positive Performance Parent**

2. Follow the **6 Parent Strategies** to play the best role for your child.

3. Watch my video, **"How to Help Your Performer Child"** in the **Book Bonus Encore Page (http://jessicaneighbor. com/book-bonuses)**

Notes

Notes

Notes

49465997R00060

Made in the USA
Middletown, DE
18 October 2017